Lifelines 28

Humphry Repton
An illustrated life of Humphry Repton
1752-1818
Kay N. Sanecki

Contents

ACKNOWLEDGEMENTS

My indebtedness is immense to those whose diligent researches have provided previous books about Humphry Repton, and I have drawn freely upon the works of Dorothy Stroud and Hugh Prince. Further, I would like to acknowledge help from the Hertfordshire County Records Office and the librarians of the Norfolk County Library and Ashridge Management College library, and thank Mr John Harvey and Mrs Phyllis Mathers, a descendant of Humphry Repton for helpful information.

Illustrations are acknowledged as follows: Studio Aemaage, page 2; Iris Hardwick, pages 26 and 37; Ruth Rutter, page 29; reproduced by kind permission of Hugh Prince from his book 'Parks in England' (Pinhorn, 1968), page 34; Kay N. Sanecki, page 47.

The cover is from Repton's Red Book for Ashridge, a detail of 'From the House and Terrace Looking South', by kind permission of Ashridge Management College.

Printed by C. I. Thomas & Sons (Haverfordwest) Ltd.

Opposite: Humphry Repton, an engraving published in 1802.

Humphry Repton

Humphry Repton's trade card. The original measured 96mm by 67mm and was usually pasted inside the front cover of his Red Books.

The man

Humphry Repton was born at Bury St Edmunds, Suffolk, on 21st April 1752, the second child of John and Martha Repton. Of their eleven children only three survived: Dorothy, born in 1747, Humphry, and a younger brother John, born in 1753. The registration of Humphry's christening at St James's church, Bury St Edmunds, on 5th May 1752 shows a mis-spelling of the family name, recorded as Ripton. His mother, reputedly beautiful and intelligent, before her marriage to John Repton was Martha Fitch of Moor Hall, Suffolk. Her ancestor, Sir Thomas Fitch, had distinguished himself in the service of Henry V and had been rewarded by the accolade of a Knight Banneret at Agincourt. John Repton was able to provide well for his family, for he was a collector of excise; his wife inherited property around the small Suffolk town of Clare. So Humphry, of optimistic and affectionate disposition and with a lively mind, responded to the congeniality of his surroundings and developed into a frank and open boy with strong creative abilities. These were to direct his life, providing him with a *raison d'être* during times of difficulty and eventually with the livelihood for which he is chiefly remembered — that of landscape architect.

He was to recall in his *Memoirs* many years later: 'It was to my early facility and love of the art of drawing, that I am indebted, not only for success in my profession, but for more than half the enjoyment of my life. When I look back to the many hundred evenings passed in the circle of my own family and drawing and representing to others what I saw in my own imagination, I may reckon this art among the most delightful of my joys.'

During Humphry's schooldays his family moved to Norwich and, having begun his education at Bury St Edmunds grammar school, he continued it at the grammar school in Norwich until he was twelve years of age.

EDUCATION IN HOLLAND

In 1764 young Humphry was plucked from the security of his home and sent to Holland to further his education. He was to go to a school owned by Mynheer Algidus Zimmerman in the village of Wokum. John Repton considered the acquisition of a second language, particularly Dutch, to be an attribute to a youth destined for a career in commerce in the flourishing city of Norwich. Trade with the Netherlands was brisk, the language the tongue of the traders. The lad and his father set sail from Harwich and disembarked at Helvoetsluys on the Dutch coast. Young Repton saw only the Dutch landscape and its gardens as compensation for the misery of his initial loneliness.

A probable business acquaintance of John Repton, Zachary Hope of Rotterdam, a member of an influential family of merchant bankers, was given the money to defray the school fees for the following two years. It was when Humphry Repton went to visit Mr Hope, possibly to thank him (as some authorities suggest), or more probably in his misery to establish contact with a remote connection with home that he was invited to stay for a day or two. Zachary Hope's home was welcoming and hospitable, his wife a warm-hearted woman, and his only son about Humphry Repton's age; it was natural for the homesick boy to prolong his visit and ultimately stay for two years. During that period Repton shared the tutors and the advantages of the well-connected Hope family, no doubt mastering Dutch and finding much to gladden his lively artistic mind in the Netherlands.

APPRENTICESHIP AND MARRIAGE

At sixteen he returned to Norwich to be apprenticed in the textile trade, to learn the mercantile qualities of lace, brocades and satins, or 'calimancoes, mecklenburgs, worsted satins' and such fabrics of the fashion and furnishing business. Perhaps for the first time his creative ability provided an outlet for his frustrations, for he seems to have displayed little aptitude, and less enthusiasm, for the trade his father had selected for him, and for which a handsome premium had been paid. The youth's interest in music (he was a flautist), his poetic turn of mind and his drawing appear to have been the crutch upon which he depended to help him through the seven years of his apprenticeship. Social life in Norwich, for the well-to-do, was full of interest, and Repton's ease of manner and natural charm ensured popularity for him.

At eighteen he fell in love with a young lady, the belle of many balls. Her name was Mary Clarke and she was to be his lifelong love and companion. Their parents objected to the marriage before Humphry was of age and, after waiting for three years, the couple were married in May 1773, immediately following his twenty-first birthday, at the church of St Mary in Marsh, Norwich. Forty years later, in writing to Mary of his happy married life, he was to say: 'I fixed my hopes where I have never been disappointed . . .' She was a retiring figure, content to govern the domestic side of the family, and bore him sixteen children, seven of whom survived to reach maturity.

About the time of their marriage Repton's father set him up in business as a general merchant in Norwich and in a house in the parish of St Giles. Only the parish register provides details of their early life together, recording the baptisms of three babies. The first was a daughter named after her paternal grandmother, Martha, born 5th March 1774 and baptised the following day, and who did not survive; the second a son, John Adey, born 29th March and baptised 1st April 1775. John Adey was so named to cement the new family connections with John Adey of Aylsham, a respected solicitor whom Humphry's sister Dorothy had recently married. The third child born while the Reptons lived in Norwich was another son, Humphry, born 3rd June 1776 and baptised five days later. He was one of four sons to survive at the time of his parents' deaths.

It was the eldest son, John Adey, who was to inherit his father's artistic ability and in spite of the isolation of deafness and bachelorhood was to outlive all his younger brothers and sisters.

Humphry Repton's success as a general merchant seems to have been quite considerable despite the fact that his heart was in his work scarcely enough to generate the enthusiasm to succeed. In 1778 an inheritance from his parents, who died within a short period of each other, confirmed his decision to abandon the world of commerce for that of country squire. Whether he intended to find an occupation more congenial to his talents and aptitude, or whether, now that his father was dead, he felt no obligation to remain in a trade for which he had little sympathy, is not known. The loss at sea of some merchant vessels with a consequent financial forfeit influenced his plans to leave the city and its business life.

7

MOVE TO THE COUNTRY

The Reptons and their two small sons moved to the village of Sustead, north of Norwich, about four miles from Aylsham where Humphry's sister, Dorothy, and her husband, John Adey, were already settled in a house bequeathed to Dorothy by her father, John Repton, and not far from Oxmead Hall which their brother John rented. Humphry Repton settled his family at Old Hall, Sustead, a red brick seventeenth-century house with Dutch gables, and there he enjoyed the pleasures of a small estate, albeit in an impecunious manner for they were forced to live simply. In the ensuing years they knew the confining influences of a limited budget and a growing family. The creative flare which Repton displayed had full rein, his early writing and interest in the theatre, his music and his sketching provided him with occupation if not with income and his serene and cheerful nature, complemented by his wife's amenable disposition, led him to describe this period of his life as 'five years of domestic bliss'.

Hindsight has shown that it was during this period that the guiding influences of his life began to play a part. One or two abortive schemes to make a living no doubt cost the young man much mental discontent, and about the end of 1783 the family moved to a much humbler property at Harestreet in Essex.

Subject to human predicament and to the demands of his growing family, he eventually resolved 'as a result of one more sleepless night' to start working as a professional landscape designer. The culmination of ten years of establishing contacts among the gentry, learning more and more of what he saw from his sketching activities and applying knowledge of plants and the countryside gleaned during the period was his decision to write to all his friends and acquaintances announcing his intention and requesting patronage. Repton said: 'I have adopted the term landscape gardening as most proper, as the art can only be perfected by the united powers of the *landscape painter* and the *practical gardener*.' The first commissions came locally, from Jeremiah Ives Esquire of Catton and from Thomas William Coke Esquire of Holkham in 1788, followed by Tofts Hall (Norfolk) for Stephen Gallwey and Hanworth (Norfolk) for Robert Lee Doughty, then Welbeck Abbey (Nottinghamshire) for the Duke of Portland, Milton (Cambridgeshire) for Samuel Knight, Crowfield (Suffolk) for William Middleton M.P., Buckenham House (Norfolk) for Lord Petre, Babergh Hall (Suffolk) for John Patteson in 1789 and Rivenhall (Essex)

Repton always considered the aspect as a whole and went to considerable pains to achieve a harmonious effect between architecture and planting. Here he illustrates the varying effect of Gothic and Classic architecture with round-headed and pointed trees. Most of the conifers of fastigiate form and various colours had not been introduced into Britain in Repton's day.

for Charles Weston. Further afield he worked at Sheffield Park (Sussex) for Lord Sheffield and Brondesburg, later Brandesburg (Middlesex) for Lady Salusbury.

By his self-confessed blessing of good health he was able in the next thirty years not only to establish himself as a fashionable consultant of the period, but to travel many hundreds of miles, produce elegant watercolour designs and meticulous descriptive proposals for his various clients, and to write several books. He also compiled a collection of manuscripts about his early life, which he left to his children. He became known as 'Mr Repton' and moved with ease and charm among the gentry, but never aspiring to a chaise of his own for his frequent professional travels. In a letter to his good friend William Windham in 1790, Repton referred to his road expenses: '. . . with the satisfaction of placing almost every day 3, 4 or 5 guineas to somebody's account, I am often under difficulty to procure ready money for road expenses — having never during the whole of this year travell'd less than 5 and 6 hundred miles each month.'

It was in a carriage accident on 29th January 1811 that Repton sustained a spinal injury from which he never recovered; the consequent lack of exercise is said to have brought on recurring angina and he and his family accepted that a stroke would probably prove fatal. His daughters were with him, returning from a ball given by Sir Thomas Lennard, when the carriage was overturned in a snowdrift. Repton was confined to his bed for many weeks, and moved with difficulty for the remaining seven years of his life. He died at breakfast, 24th March 1818, at his home in Harestreet, Essex, which in spite of his increasing wealth over the years he had never left. Mary Repton survived her husband by nine years and died on 6th April 1827. She was buried with him in a plot he had chosen against the south wall of the parish church of Aylsham, St Michael Archangel, a church founded by John of Gaunt. The tomb is enclosed by a rail and has been restored recently. Humphry Repton wrote these lines as his own epitaph:

> Not like Egyptian Tyrants consecrate,
> Unmixed with others shall my dust remain;
> But mold'ring, blending, melting into Earth,
> Mine shall give form and colour to the Rose;
> And while its vivid blossoms cheer Mankind,
> Its perfumed odours shall ascend to Heaven.

Pater familias

Humphry Repton was thirty-six years of age when he embarked upon his career as a landscape gardener; the previous ten years, though unremunerative, had been formative. The early days at Sustead were passed in managing his own holding as thriftily as possible and in sketching the various homes of the landed gentry and nobility in the surrounding parts of Norfolk.

William Windham of Felbrigg was his neighbour at Sustead — Felbrigg Hall lies just across the fields. Windham was a scholarly man who was building up an extensive library which Repton enjoyed. They shared the same literary tastes and were contemporaries — Windham was but two years Repton's junior. After being educated at Eton and Oxford William Windham had made the Grand Tour and returned with a remarkable collection of Busiri's landscape paintings (which are still to be seen at Felbrigg). Much time was spent together in the library on the upper floor, and their compatible taste and love of literature no doubt provided a common interest. Windham is said to have preferred the rough and tumble of Repton's overcrowded family life to his own elegant surroundings at Felbrigg, and to have suffered the changeable mood of a depressive intellectual nature. Repton's optimistic and constantly cheerful outlook complemented their relationship and friendship. In the election of 1780 Repton acted as Windham's agent, and although Windham was not returned Repton valued the experience and occupation for he was to recall in later years in a correspondence with William Windham: 'My services at the last election which you are pleased to remember with so much generosity of sentiment and with such nice distinction in the value of my time, you have already bought and paid for in the advantage I derive from the honour of your friendship which I am fully sensible is my best introduction wherever I am call'd in professionally . . .' This letter was written when in spite of having several demanding commissions as a landscape gardener Repton acted as agent for William

11

Windham in the Norwich election of 1790 organising the supplies of hand-bills, transport, banners and refreshment.

A POST IN IRELAND

Repton's lack of funds kept him at home at Sustead, but Windham was a well-connected wit of the period and no doubt related much news of his activities to his friend. Repton clearly made several valuable acquaintances at Felbrigg. In 1783 William Windham was asked to become Chief Secretary to the Earl of Northington upon his appointment as Lord Lieutenant of Ireland. Once Repton had the news that his friend had accepted the invitation he wrote to Windham asking if there might be the possibility of some employment for him attendant upon the office. Windham replied: 'It happens, very whimsically, that your proposal is just an echo to a wish I was about to express to you . . . If you, as soon as it is convenient, will come to town, you may be of great immediate use to me: and we can then more conveniently talk over matters.' Windham confessed in the same letter that he was not 'over happy' and 'having got myself into a scrape, my first thought was how I might bring my friends in with me; and in that light I had very early designs on you.' Ireland had supposedly acquired legislative independence in the previous year, and in the so-called 'Grattan's Parliament' the administration was in the hands of a Lord Lieutenant appointed by the British Government. Repton's role took him right to the helm of Anglo-Irish politics. The Court of the Lord Lieutenant was more amusing and opulent than that of London; life at the Castle in Dublin was lively and Repton's easy charm was an asset in the situation. He stayed with Sarah Siddons who was appearing at the New Theatre in Smock Alley, one of Dublin's two commodious theatres, in Garrick's play *Isabella*. Repton knew her previously, for his interest in the theatre was strong and she was a friend of many well-connected people. There is little doubt, however, that their acquaintanceship continued, for some time later Humphry Repton addressed one of his poems to her and it was published subsequently in *Odd Whims* (1804). The vigour and ease with which Repton embraced the life in Dublin was not shared by Windham — who had had his misgivings in the first place; he found the tedium of the Castle and parliamentary procedure confining in the extreme after his broader horizons and his Norfolk estates, London politics and intellectual pursuits. He was not in sympathy with his principal, Lord

Northington, who administered in a spirit of concession to popular claims in Ireland where, even more than in eighteenth-century England, the extremes of poverty and splendour clashed, inflaming the already explosive Irish resentment of English rule. When Windham was sent back to London on a parliamentary assignment he tendered his resignation to the Prime Minister, William Pitt. His return to Dublin was prevented by illness and it fell to Humphry Repton to clear up Windham's affairs, both the official business and outstanding private matters. He remained for six weeks, working with Lord Northington, and in correspondence with Windham he wrote: 'My Lord Lieutenant has very charitably since your absence been pleased to take much notice of me.' The landscape gardens

A watercolour with Repton's caption: 'Epping Forest with Mr Knight cutting our joint names — very low forest car & Captain'.

The view from the Reptons' cottage at Harestreet, Essex, which Humphry Repton set about improving.

of Ireland provided Repton with new ideas, and his meetings with landscapists to whom he was introduced by the Archbishop of Armagh must have filled his spare time.

MOVE TO ESSEX

His return to England, by means of the packet-boat to Holyhead, was announced in a letter to Mary Repton at the end of August: 'And now, my dearest Mary, what have I been doing? I have learned to love my home; I have gained some knowledge of the world; some of the public business, and some of hopeless expectancies; I have made some valuable acquaintances; I have formed some connections with the great; I have seen a fine country, in passing through Wales, and have made some sketches; I have lost very little money; I shall have got the brogue; and you will have got a tabinet gown. So ends my Irish expedition.' Revealing in the extreme Repton's ability to recognise the advantages in a situation and to take the optimistic view, this letter gives no hint of his diminishing funds, nor does it express any

14

The garden at Harestreet was extended to include the small village green, and the butcher's shop was obscured — a simple but effective treatment.

resentment at Windham's decision to leave Ireland. The decision to move to a smaller house was imminent. Almost as soon as he returned home, in spite of the expected birth of another child, the Reptons made plans to move to Harestreet, near Romford, to a somewhat inelegant cottage close to a fairly busy highway. That a man so closely associated with his family should leave the nucleus in northern Norfolk and settle in Essex without work to go to is perplexing, but Repton obviously sought the proximity of London and the available connections in the hope of work. After the rural situation of their home at Sustead this was a retrograde step for the family, but Humphry set about 'improving' the outlook from the windows of the cottage by incorporating a little more land within the hedge from the rough triangle beyond. He erected a treillage to support roses to obscure the butcher's shop window, while retaining the view of the attractive roof of the same premises. About the time of the move to this cottage another son was born. Repton's acceptance without complaint of the reversal of his good fortune occasioned by Wind-

15

ham's return to England reveals the philosophical serenity of his nature and amid the upheaval of the ensuing reorganisation of his family he called his son William, possibly after William Windham. Twenty-three years later this same son was to succeed his uncle, John Adey, as a solicitor in Aylsham, and seek the patronage of William Windham, somewhat unsuccessfully.

The following year, 1784, Windham was elected to represent Norwich, a seat he held for eighteen years, and Repton involved himself in politics once again, organising the campaign. Writing of this period to Windham some years later, Humphry Repton said: 'When I on a former occasion reveal'd to you the unpleasant position of my affairs, my affliction arose rather from dread of poverty than from its actual pressure and now (1790) my happiness proceeds rather from a hope of future affluence . . . than from actual riches in my possession.'

A SCHEME FOR SAFER MAIL-COACHES

In 1778 Sarah Siddons, who had been a strolling actress and an utter failure in her appearance for Garrick at Drury Lane, accepted an offer from John Palmer, manager of the Theatre Royal in Bath, to play the role of Elwina in Hannah More's tragedy *Percy*. The critical audiences in the spa went wild with enthusiasm for her performance and Mrs Siddons was established as an actress. Her grateful friendliness towards John Palmer continued and when he was looking for a designer who could further his ideas for the improved safety of the mail-coaches, Repton was approached, doubtless as a result of his acquaintance with Sarah Siddons and Ralph Allen of Prior Park.

It was an official precaution against robbery in the 1770s to dispatch in halves banknotes and bills of exchange sent by mail. Palmer advocated faster purpose-built coaches, accompanied by an armed guard. The first coaches were run in August 1784. Repton, fired with enthusiasm for the scheme, invested his small capital in it. It would appear that his trusting nature failed to prompt him to draw up some business-like agreement for the ensuing revenue; he certainly did not share in the substantial financial rewards which the Palmer family received. John Palmer himself was appointed by William Pitt to be controller-general of postal revenues, and on vacating the post obtained a pension of £3,000 a year and by an Act of Parliament in 1813 a sum of £50,000.

A design for a transparency by Repton. George III's head surmounts an armed mail coach such as was envisaged by John Palmer, with whom Repton worked on this project.

This second dashing of Repton's hopes was followed by three or four years of an apparently desultory way of life in which he continued to sketch, often at home in the evening while Mary read to him, and to write. He wrote a comedy, *Odd Whims or Two at a Time*, which Windham gave to Edmund Burke to read; because of his pleasure in it Burke passed it on to Sir Joshua Reynolds, who mislaid the manuscript. It was not until 1804 that *Odd Whims* was published together with a collection of essays from *Variety*, the work of Repton and some of his friends, first prepared in 1788.

FRIENDS AND ACQUAINTANCES

Most authorities refer to Sir James Edward Smith as a school friend of Humphry Repton, but as Repton was his senior by seven years and left Norwich at thirteen to go to Holland, it seems more likely that they became acquainted in Norwich during Repton's apprenticeship. James

Edward was the son of James Smith who kept a woollen draper's shop in Gentleman's Way near St Peter Mancroft church in Norwich. Repton was apprenticed to a kindred trade and both he and James Edward Smith had a boyhood interest in botany. Smith was to found the Linnean Society of London in 1788 (the year Repton resolved to become a landscape gardener) and be the Founder President for forty years. He was a close friend of Sir Joseph Banks, President of the Royal Society. Repton also knew Banks, having been introduced to him by William Windham. While there is no evidence that Humphry Repton was in the same social circles as these men and their fraternity, even later in life when success had presented him to some of the foremost personages, he no doubt knew many of their contemporaries: such men as William Forsyth, formerly gardener to King George III at Kensington and St James's, then to the Duke of Northumberland at Syon House and from 1770 Curator of Chelsea Physic Garden; and James Dickson, a nurseryman and seedsman of Covent Garden, who together with Forsyth, Banks and others founded the Horticultural Society (now the Royal Horticultural Society) in 1804. James Dickson had the rare distinction of being a founder member of both the Linnean Society and the Horticultural Society.

Another neighbour at home was Robert Marsham of Stratton Strawless, from whom Repton learned an enormous amount about trees and shrubs, crop husbandry, weather, ornithology and entomology. Although Robert Marsham was nearly fifty years Humphry Repton's senior their common interest in natural history was the bond that spanned the generation gap. A third friend was Benjamin Stillingfleet, who had been tutor to William Windham. In 1780 Robert Marsham was elected to the Royal Society, at the age of seventy-two, having contributed several papers on tree growth to the Society's *Transactions*. It was about this time that he imposed upon Humphry Repton to edit an extensive manuscript on gardening. Not only was Repton able to persuade him to alter some of the eccentric ideas he had propounded, but eventually to abandon the idea of publication rather than subject himself to the 'ridicule of an unkindly world'.

Thus in 1788 when Repton embarked upon his career as a landscape gardener it was upon these people and their friends and acquaintances that he depended, and the knowledge and experience gained provided the platform from which he was able to proclaim his intentions.

The landscape gardener

His first commission came in 1788 from a friend of William Windham, Jeremiah Ives, at Norwich. He was building a villa for himself at Catton, a village on the outskirts of the city, and Repton worked there on the virgin site of 112 acres. At Holkham, Norfolk, the same year he was commissioned by Thomas William Coke, later the first Earl of Leicester, another friend of William Windham and a respected colleague of Repton, for Repton was at that time engaged in political activities on behalf of Coke. With how much confidence Repton approached this work is not known, but the building at Holkham was already famous as the first designed by William Kent, and both he and Capability Brown had landscaped the park.

THE RED BOOKS

From the beginning Repton applied his skill as a water-colourist and writer in explaining his proposals to his clients. This he did in the form of a 'Red Book'; a volume handsomely bound in red Moroccan leather with gold tooling and about 12 by 9 inches in size. Within, his persuasive and respectful style of description must have opened up new realms to many people who were to consider the ideas, for Repton not only drew the attention to many details of environment and aspect, but presented a visual representation of the completed scheme. He devised a folded flap (or in some instances, flaps) as an overlay which when lifted showed the scene as it would be. Some of these Red Books have survived, but the existence of such a volume for an estate does not necessarily mean that the work was carried out. The Red Books were merely highly individual specifications.

The Red Book which Repton prepared in 1788 for T. W. Coke at Holkham is the earliest to remain on its 'home ground'. The only earlier one had been for Brandesburg (no Red Book was prepared for Sheffield Park); this was sold to a collector at Sotheby's in 1957. The Holkham book was delivered in the autumn of 1789. Work began at

19

Repton suggested removing parts of the formal garden at Lathom, Lancs (top). By demolishing the pool, reflected light would not interfere with the view beyond (centre: with the flap lifted from the top picture). (Below) the resulting landscape, showing the effect of removing the water, bringing the landscape nearer the house.

20

Holkham before the year ended. His mechanical skill and in-ventiveness was brought to bear, for in preference to a bridge Repton contrived for the lake a ferry-boat which could 'be managed with the greatest of ease by any Lady'.

By the following spring Repton was equipping himself with the tools of his trade, a theodolite and level, possibly because he had had further commissions promised. Miss Stroud in *Humphry Repton* (1962) records that Repton wrote at this time to Robert Marsham: 'I know it will give you pleasure to hear in my delightful profession I meet with all the success my hopes could flatter me with.'

ABUNDANT COMMISSIONS

The next major commission came from the Duke of Portland at Welbeck, Nottinghamshire, for which three Red Books in all were prepared as the work progressed, the last not until 1803, by which time his client was Lord Titchfield for the Duke of Portland had made over the estate to his son. Welbeck Abbey had come into the family when the Duke's father had married Margaret, heiress of the Duke of Newcastle, but his favourite home was his estate in Buckinghamshire, Bulstrode near Gerrards Cross. It was here that he took Repton to work on the park in 1790; this led to other commissions in that county and neighbouring Hertfordshire, Bedfordshire and Berkshire: Wyddial Hall, Little Court and Lamer in Hertfordshire, 1790; Hasells in Bedfordshire for Francis Pym the same year, and then in 1793 and 1794 Gayhurst, Tyringham, and, in the extreme north of Buckinghamshire, and within a year or so, the nearby Hanslope Park. Other commissions at Thoresby, Grove and Milton possibly came in the wake of work at Welbeck.

Whether Repton worked first at Tyringham or the adjoining Gayhurst is not clear but William Praed, having demolished his Elizabethan mansion at Tyringham in 1792, was building a smaller classical house, designed by John Soane, and called in Repton to landscape the park. There is nothing obviously of Repton's signature on the estate today; the Indianesque water garden designed by Sir Edwin Lutyens is probably unique in England now. Repton's main alteration was to construct a glade from Gayhurst on to the Tyringham estate; a glade that now swoops in derelict beauty under the Newport Pagnell-Northampton road (A50) at Gayhurst village. The site of a

Roman chalybeate spring, now no longer rich in iron, and a reservoir probably inspired Repton to enhance this ride of established use. Known as 'Sir Everard Digby's Walk' long before Humphry Repton came on the scene, its romantic historical association has been perpetuated. From the lawn at the back of the E-shaped Elizabethan mansion of Gayhurst a path enfolded by the tunnel-like growth of yew leads across the estate to the walk which Repton altered, and it was here that Sir Everard and his fellow-conspirators of the Gunpowder Plot had walked and hidden.

Repton was several times to draw upon history to provide a design appropriate to its location. Most notably, at Ashridge he contrived an elaborate 'holy well' or conduit, homage to the monastic Bonhommes of the thirteenth century. In *Sketches and Hints* he says, in speaking of the associations a garden may enfold, 'whether excited by local accident . . . by the remains of antiquity, . . . but more particularly by that personal attachment to long known objects . . .' that 'such partialities should be respected and indulged, since true taste, which is generally attended by great sensibility, ought to be the guardian of it in others.'

From the north Buckinghamshire locations he was called to the banks of the Thames in Berkshire, where new houses were being constructed at Holme Park and Coombe, and at nearby Purley the old house was being replaced. Simultaneously Repton was supervising work in Nottinghamshire, possibly stemming from the original commission at Welbeck Abbey, at Thoresby and Buckminster, both in 1791. In East Anglia he worked at Bracondale for Philip Martineau, a Norwich surgeon, in 1792, and Honing Hall for Thomas Cubitt in the same year. Clearly this commission pleased him; all his suggestions were not executed but at least some were and before him both Brown and John Soane had been consulted by Thomas Cubitt and the landscape had been left in peace, nature's hand considered better than man's. It was in the Red Book for Honing that Repton wrote: 'There is hardly any part of England in which I am less known professionally than in Norfolk, perhaps from it being "the Prophet's own country".' That the park should seemingly be one and the same with the surrounding countryside had been part of 'Capability' Brown's philosophy and Repton endeavoured at this stage in his career to achieve the same end. In the same Red Book he said: 'With respect to its (the park's) size there is one invariable rule, viz. it must appear to

Michael Grove, Sussex, (above) as it was when Repton was called in. The overlay lifted (below) reveals how he envisaged it: a wing rebuilt, the terrace wall added, the estate road cleared away and the landscape 'animated' with animals. However, the owner's sudden death prevented the implementation of these plans.

have no boundary.' This could be accomplished in various ways such as by the removal of fences or hedges or by the planting of a screen of trees. At Honing he went so far as to suggest that a nearby mill be purchased so that a rural tower could be sited upon it as an eye catcher.

With his practical experience now established and satisfied clients giving favourable reports (if not settling their accounts) Humphry Repton quite naturally started to write his first book on the subject about this time. *Sketches and Hints on Landscape Gardening* was written with these early commissions accomplished, though it had a halting progress to publication in 1795. Meanwhile William Pitt, whom Repton knew through William Windham and his other political connections, consulted him about the grounds of Holmwood House in Kent where he was anxious to make further improvements. The house has since been replaced by one designed by Decimus Burton but considerable portions of the original landscape are still to be seen. Repton's first work in Kent had been at Langley Park for Sir Peter Burrel in 1790, but the patronage of William Pitt was to open many opportunities, for although 1790 and 1791 had been busy years for the newly established landscape architect with journeys to the Midlands, the West Country and the North-west he had not hitherto been to Cornwall. Pitt's brother-in-law was Lord Eliot of Port Eliot near St Germans, Cornwall, and, although Repton admitted that a better hand than his had already fashioned the aspect of the land there and that it benefited from proximity to the sea, he had established a foothold in the county, chiefly among the landed political supporters of Pitt.

METHODS AND THEORIES

Not infrequently very little change was made to an existing park; Repton seems never to have assumed responsibility for mighty changes of contour, but rather he exercised restraint. It was at Port Eliot that he said: 'Like the conquered magician I break my wand in the presence of superior skill.' And later (1800) at West Wycombe in Buckinghamshire he advised merely the removal of an existing clump of trees on the island to reveal the clear outline of the pavilion. In 1799 when considering Tewin Water, Hertfordshire, he wrote in the Red Book: 'A large tree in every situation is too respectable an object to be

Digression

A page from the Red Book for Panshanger, Hertfordshire, in which Repton digresses to discuss the effect of light.

hastily sacrificed especially in compliance with the fashion of the day. A better reason than fashion must be advanced for cutting down large trees.' He was at that point putting forward reasons for allowing seventeenth-century avenues to remain.

The immensity of scale of the panorama on which a landscape gardener of the eighteenth-century worked must have required an intrinsic stage-craft. Repton gave his sources of pleasure to be considered in *Sketches and Hints*; picturesque effect, intricacy, simplicity, variety, novelty, contrast, continuity, association, grandeur, appropriation, animation, and the seasons and time of day. Constantly he referred to the value of light, the changed atmosphere of the aspect from one season to another, or from morning to evening. In the Red Book for Panshanger there are two watercolour sketches depicting the same scene of river, cattle and cottage, the one in the morning the other in the evening light. These illustrations appear in *Theory and*

Practice and Repton recalls 'a curious observation which occurred in the view of the Thames at Purley'. Thus he has used previously acquired knowledge as an example and the view depicted does not pertain to Panshanger but to Purley where he worked nine years earlier. An extreme instance of the effect of light was considered for Lathom, Lancashire, where the Red Book shows the effect of removing the pond near the house 'which is so near the eye that its glare prevents the lawn from being seen beyond it'. Adverse qualities, to be avoided in creating a homogeneous whole, he listed as congruity, utility, order and symmetry, adding: 'the cultivated mind is shocked by such things as would not be visible to the clown.'

A commission came from Lord Berwick in 1797 to landscape the park around his recently built classical house at Attingham, Shropshire, and by recommending that the river Tern be cleared of its reedy margin and cattle grazed to enliven the scene Repton accomplished the reproduction of the most natural of landscapes. A considerable amount of work was to follow in the western part of the country: Brentry (Gloucestershire) for William Payne in 1802; Dyrham Park (Gloucestershire) in 1801-3; Condover Hall and Hopton Court, 1803 and Longnor Hall, 1804, all in Shropshire; Hooton Hall (Cheshire) 1803; and Stanage (Radnorshire) 1803.

Meanwhile work was in progress as far afield as Harewood House, Yorkshire, for Lord Harewood, Cassiobury Park, Hertfordshire, Bayham in Kent and Betchworth in Surrey.

At Harewood House in 1800 Repton arrived to see planting some thirty years old designed by Capability Brown and was commissioned to 'improve' the park. A new gateway and a carriageway were designed but much of Repton's work there was subsequently obliterated by the formal terraces designed by Sir Charles Barry. The gateway, the design of which Repton was particularly proud of, was changed considerably and erected in a position less favourable to its purpose and the scheme as a whole than he had intended. Some of his sketches hang in the exhibition room of Harewood. At Cassiobury (then known as Cashiobury) on the outskirts of Watford the Earl of Essex had had his house rebuilt under the supervision of James Wyatt and Repton

Opposite: Attingham Park, Salop, where much work was carried out by Nash, and where Repton laid out the park around the river Tern for Lord Berwick about 1798.

27

cleared some of the ancient trees, opening up the undulating land-scape watered by the river Gade.

In 1800 the Duke of Bedford obtained an act of Parliament for the development of his London estates and Humphry Repton prepared the designs for the planting within Russell Square. The walk in the square culminated in the bronze statue commemorating Francis, fifth Duke of Bedford, by Richard Westmacott, unveiled in 1809, four years after the Duke's death. The statue pays tribute to his interest in agriculture, for he is shown with one hand on the plough and the other holding an ear of corn. On his estates in Bedfordshire the Duke had run a model farm and in the park at Woburn Repton carried out various garden embellishments, including a flower corridor, a rosary, American garden, Chinese garden, menagerie and improvements to a drive. The stone bridge which carries the drive over a small valley is now failing under the weight of tourist traffic. In *Fragments* Repton says that nowhere were the improvements he had proposed 'so fully realised as at Woburn Abbey'. The Duke of Bedford's further requests were for a lodge, which still stands, at Apsley Wood on the Woburn estate, and for the laying out of the grounds at his Devon home, Endsleigh near Tavistock. A house was built there by Wyattville, starting in 1810, and it seems likely that Repton visited the site prior to his carriage ac-cident, but not afterwards; the work was supervised by John Adey.

The return to flower gardens as a decorative feature within sight of the house was becoming apparent during the first decade of the nineteenth century and Repton indulged this taste noticeably at Woburn, in his proposals for Brighton, and later at Ashridge in Hertfordshire (but at that time in Buckinghamshire).

ASHRIDGE

In *Fragments* in 1816 Repton wrote of Ashridge: 'of all the subjects on which I have been consulted few have excited so much interest in my mind as the plan for these gardens . . . it being the youngest favourite, the child of my age and declining power; when no longer able to undertake the more extensive plans of landscape. I was glad to

Opposite: Francis, fifth Duke of Bedford, one of Repton's patrons. This bronze statue stands in Russell Square, London.

FRANCIS
DUKE OF BEDFORD.

ERECTED

MDCCCIX.

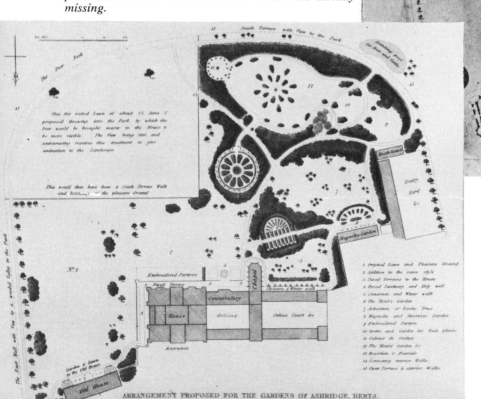

Opposite: A plan of Ashridge, Hertfordshire, after the flower gardens had been made, published by Todd in 1821. Repton's general design had been followed.

Below: Repton's interpretation from memory of his proposals for the garden at Ashridge, Hertfordshire, published in 1816 when the Red Book was already missing.

ARRANGEMENT PROPOSED FOR THE GARDENS OF ASHRIDGE, HERTS.

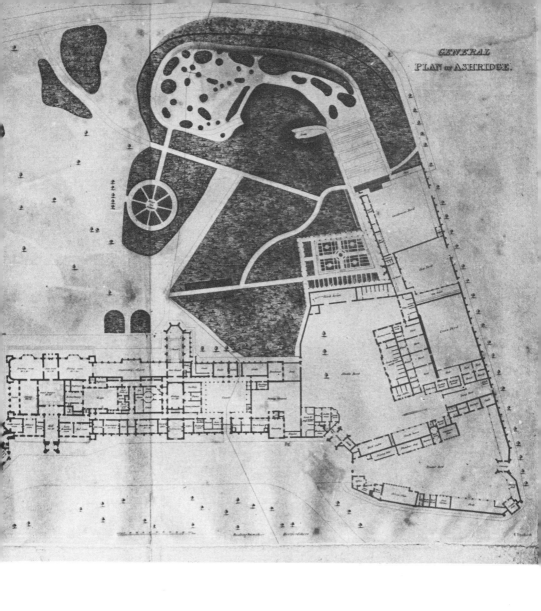

contract my views within the narrow circle of a garden independent of its accompaniment of distant scenery'. James Wyatt was building a Gothic pile for the Earl of Bridgewater (started in 1809) and Repton was consulted in 1813 concerning the layout of the pleasure grounds to the south of the new house. The diary of William Buckingham, the estate bailiff, records the visits of the Reptons, father and son, during the spring and early summer of that year: (25th March)'Ld & Ly B to London brot Repton down and back same evening'. Presumably Repton delivered his proposals in the Red Book, for on 31st March the Earl of Bridgewater lent it to Buckingham to examine and the evening was passed in 'looking at Mr Repton's drawings then at newspapers'. By Easter, when Lord Clive was a visitor, Humphry and John Adey Repton arrived at Ashridge and both stayed; on 22nd April they were in the gardens, as the diary records: '. . .to the pleasure grounds to Ld & Ly B, Mr Repton & Son, Hemmings & Jarvis, respecting work'. The following day 'Ld B: young Mr Repton left at ½ past 2'. There is no reference as to when Humphry Repton left but he returned on Sunday 6th June and, when on the following Friday a 'Perambulation of the Parish' took place, Repton was still there and joined Lord and Lady Bridgewater to meet the participants, 'then on to Lt. Gad (Little Gaddesden) & the Park Ld B met us there and Ly B & Repton . . .'

By the time Humphry Repton was writing *Fragments* (1816) the Red Book he had prepared for Ashridge was missing. He wrote: 'I delivered my opinion, enriched by many drawings some of which have since been realised, and with some I had hoped to enrich this volume; but I am informed, the book has been mislaid and I can therefore only describe the general principles of what I had the honour to suggest . . .' However, Repton drew from his memory of the original proposals and the notes are added in the past tense. Other sketches made at the same time show the rosary and a conduit which was to be constructed in cast iron — a material new for decorative purposes at the time. The rosary was built in a slightly simpler form and the general plan remains today. The conduit was also simplified, by Wyatville, and was installed in a different position; it was cleaned and restored in the 1960s. One interesting fact that Repton confirms in *Fragments* is that he suggested forming the grotto as 'an excavation formed out of an old pool instead of filling it up'. The grotto was subsequently constructed in this way using Hertfordshire pudding stone.

By 1821 Todd was writing his description of the new house and garden and said: 'As far as the garden has been described, the original idea and design of it were suggested by the late Mr Repton; which yet in many respects were varied by the directions of the Earl and Countess of Bridgewater.' Todd appends the plan which proves the simplified execution of Repton's ideas.

Clearly Repton enjoyed preparing the Red Book for Ashridge, which has subsequently been found and was sold at Sotheby's in 1971, and is in the hands of a private collector in London. The design was possible because of the enclosed level site. The intricacy of accommodating no fewer than ten smaller gardens into the plan suggests that Repton enjoyed the paper work itself; the moving away from the great spread of the landscape palette heralds the more intimate colourful gardens of the coming Victorian era. After his work at Ashridge, Repton was in declining health and no further major works were carried out; a few drawings were prepared in conjunction with John Repton, some of which schemes were not even executed.

A few years earlier in planning Russell Square (c. 1806), Cadogan Square (c. 1806) and Bloomsbury Square (c. 1807) in London he had hinted at the coming Victorian penchant for open spaces in cities and towns; though the planning of a garden in these residential squares was in no measure comparable with the public parks which were to follow.

William Buckingham's diary on 31st March 1813 records that, after his daily round as bailiff to the Earl of Bridgewater, he looked at 'Mr Repton's drawings, then at Newspapers'.

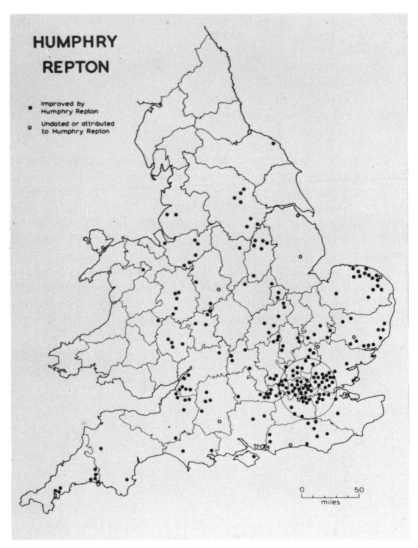

The distribution of properties improved by Humphry Repton. In less than thirty years he worked on 220 places.

The architect

Dorothy Stroud says: 'In time he (Repton) mastered a sufficient knowledge to be able to write in *The Theory* that he had made architecture a branch of his own profession, but the preparation of the necessary drawings added greatly to the mass of work already on his hands.' In the beginning he had been dependent upon the services of an able draughtsman turned architect, William Wilkins of Norwich, an acquaintance of long standing and a man who was clearly content within his craft to accept payment for his work, not seeking the publicity Repton's connections may have brought. When John Adey, Repton's eldest son, was eighteen he became a pupil of Wilkins; despite his deafness he was a scholarly lad who had inherited his father's literary predilections. Three years later, in 1795, Repton's career veered sharply towards the inclusion of architecture in his schemes, when more than ever he not only considered house and site as a unit but advised upon the buildings themselves.

PARTNERSHIP WITH NASH

Repton had previously been closely associated with the Wyatts but during the early 1790s he had encountered John Nash in the course of his journeys, most probably in the West Country. Repton had worked at Stoke Edith, Garnons and Sufton, and visited Richard Payne Knight at his splendid estate at Downton Castle which was well known to and admired by Nash. The two men reached a professional agreement; a financial arrangement was initiated, Repton's son became Nash's assistant and Nash himself returned to London and set up an office in Duke Street. John Nash had already been consulted in 1793 by Paul Cobb Methuen concerning an extension to the north front of his home, Corsham Court, Wiltshire, and by 1796 both he and Repton were undertaking their first joint commission. It appears that Wyatt had expected to undertake the alterations to the house, as

35

Nash's original proposals had been unacceptable to Mr Methuen, but Repton, already with a foothold by 1795, somehow may have persuaded his client that Nash was the preferable architect. Wyatt was paid off, refused an interview, and when rot was discovered in timbers twelve years later understandably he ignored any appeal to give an opinion. Over a period of four years or so work continued, in a seemingly desultory fashion by Nash who was widely engaged elsewhere, and on a grand scale by Repton. Once again Repton's respectfully easy manner and his essential professionalism gained a further crop of commissions in the district. Nash, on the other hand, was an ebullient little man, with probably not the same allegiance to integrity that Repton held. Nevertheless, Corsham was their first joint effort and in the ensuing two or three years the work of Nash and Repton was complementary, with a growing acceptance of classical architecture rather than the then fashionable Gothic style which Wyatt was employing. Repton wrote at length contrasting the merits and demerits of Gothic against classical styles, remarking upon size, situation and view of the buildings. He tended, he said with Milton, to favour round-headed trees to accompany Gothic-style buildings:

'Towers and battlements he sees,
Embosom'd high in tufted trees'

and provided accompanying sketches to make his point.

The partnership between Nash and Repton continued, each at the same time working independently elsewhere when the occasion arose. At Sunbridge Park, Kent, (now a management college) Repton supervised the preparation of the ideal site for the house by cutting into the hillside for some thirty feet, then John Nash was responsible for the building. Similarly in 1799 at Luscombe, South Devon, Repton was consulted on the laying out of a new estate bought by Charles Hoare and called in Nash as the architect for the Castle. There is a singular lack of evidence that Humphry Repton gained any reciprocal benefit from his partnership and by 1799, when he was invited to advise on the Hertfordshire estates of Lord Cowper, it was his son John who collaborated with him. The sweeping broad valley of the Mimram at Panshanger appealed to Repton; he visualised a broader area of water there and set to work without delay on forming a string of lakes. When the Red Book was presented in February 1800 it included two sketches for a house, the one Gothic and the alternative classical in

Corsham Court, Wiltshire, where Humphry Repton and John Nash carried out their first major joint project, for Paul Methuen.

design. Was this an attempt to establish an ability to satisfy a client without Nash's professional opinion or to promulgate the skill of his son? Or was it that Repton's tolerance of Nash was waning? Whatever the motive, it was the first hint that all was not well with the partnership between Repton and Nash. In *The Theory* Repton referred to the change of heart by writing: 'His name (John Adey's) has hitherto been little known as an architect, because it was suppressed in many works begun in that of another person to whom I freely, unreservedly and confidentially gave my advice and assistance, while my son aided, with his architectural knowledge and his pencil, to form plans and designs, from which we have derived neither fame nor profit.'

It would appear that both the Reptons felt some dissatisfaction in their working relationship with Nash and probably neither was prepared to continue subjecting themselves to hard usage. John, it must be remembered, was deaf and may well have sought the more considerate temperament of his father than the harsher conditions of Nash's practice. The estrangement may not have been, at its core, between Humphry Repton and Nash but between John Repton and Nash, for very shortly afterwards a younger brother, one of the twins, George Stanley, was taken on as an assistant by Nash.

ROYAL PATRONAGE AND THE BRIGHTON PAVILION

That Humphry Repton honoured his agreement with John Nash and introduced him to his clients brought about royal patronage for Nash. In 1797 Repton supervised alterations to the grounds of the 'marine pavilion' at Brighton for the Prince of Wales. Henry Holland (Capability Brown's son-in-law) had built a bow-fronted house in the classical style, surmounted by a shallow dome, and here the Prince spent much time — the sea water at Brighton supposedly improving his health. The Windsor archives, George IV's accounts, record

The proposed enfilade at Brighton. The corridors were to run at right angles with a mirror set in such a way that the reflection gave the appearance of one long winter garden. The windows were to be removed in summer.

The proposed view from the private apartments at Brighton. Large basket-like containers filled with plants were to provide colour at all seasons.

payments to Repton between 1797 and 1802 for work at Brighton, though the precise identity of his work there has not been established. Nash soon provided the design for a conservatory at Brighton but for Repton the story was somewhat different; Nash skimmed the cream and gained other royal commissions including the making of Regent Street and Regents Park. He was eventually to reshape the Pavilion at Brighton, in spite of Repton's plans for it being acceptable at first to the Prince of Wales.

In 1806 Repton presented plans for the reshaping of the Pavilion and gardens which delighted his royal client. 'Mr Repton,' he said, 'I consider the whole of this work as perfect, and will have every part of it carried into immediate execution, not a tittle shall be altered — even you yourself shall not attempt any improvement.' The designs were prepared with the assistance of both his sons, John Adey and George

Stanley, in the Indianesque style. Repton had been deeply impressed by the riding school to the north-west of the Pavilion at Brighton, built in this style by William Pordon who had worked with S. P. Cockerell, the architect of the newly built Sezincote in Gloucestershire. Humphry Repton had been consulted over Daniell's designs for this exotic building at Sezincote and clearly considered the Indianesque style to be the advanced fashion of the day. After his close connection with the designs of Daniell from Sezincote, Repton said 'I was pleased at having discovered new sources of beauty and variety,' and he obviously took tremendous pleasure from adapting the existing buildings at Brighton into some totality of a new style. The royal 'Red Book' now in the library at Windsor, was a large folio volume of very different format from other Red Books. The Prince of Wales in his pleasure with the proposals gave permission for it to be published in 1808. The text is accompanied by some very attractive vignettes and Humphry Repton emerges as an architect of palaces able to marry the surrounding garden site to their appropriate splendour. The proposed gardens were flower gardens, pheasantry, a sunken pool, a flower corridor or enfilade set at right angles — possibly reminiscent of the curved conservatory he knew at Sezincote, and plans to provide flowers all year round.

Repton made a long dissertation on different basic principles of Greek, Gothic and Indian architecture, accompanied by detailed illustrations. He wrote 'in works of art we can only use the *forms* of nature not the *exactness* . . . in the part taken from the vegetable kingdom to enrich the ornaments of Architecture imitation goes no farther than the general forms since we scarcely know the individual plant, although some writers have mentioned the Reed, the Acanthus and the Lotus. The *Gothic* are derived from *bud* and *germ*, the *Grecian* from the *leaf* and the *Indian* from the *flower*; a singular coincidence which seems to mark that these three styles are and ought to be kept perfectly distinct.'

The pride of the Reptons must have ridden on the crest of the waves when the Prince of Wales expressed his pleasure in their work, but the royal finances took a plunge and the work was postponed. Years later Nash was commissioned to rebuild the Pavilion and the work of Repton was absorbed into the structure. In his highest aspirations Humphry Repton worked for his royal patron and it took several years of diminishing hopes before he was to discover that Nash had captured the prize. Repton never again used the Indianesque style, but posterity owes the raffish interpretation of it at Brighton to Nash, based upon the inspiration of Humphry Repton.

Royal patronage did, however, lead to Repton's commission from Sir Harry Featherstonhaugh at Uppark in Sussex in 1805. Sir Harry was a close friend of the Prince who used to drive over from Brighton to Uppark. A single-storey addition running the entire length of the north front of the building was added, together with a new entrance. On the estate an approach road from Harting was built to the court in front of the new entrance. Further alterations were carried out about 1810 and interrupted by Repton's carriage accident and it seems fairly certain that the work was mainly supervised by John Adey.

Repton's proposal for the west front of the Pavilion at Brighton, taken from 'Designs for the Pavillon at Brighton' (1808).

An illustration from 'Designs for the Pavillon at Brighton' depicting Flora cherishing Winter. Repton was advocating all-the-year interest in the garden.

42

The writer

Throughout his life Repton indulged in the creative art of writing and broadly there were three main periods of activity. During the early years at Sustead and Harestreet he wrote essays and poems, acted as an art critic and editor and wrote a play. During the early 1800s when several projects seemed to be abortive he turned to writing and after his accident he set down his memoirs for his family and produced his most valuable works for posterity. But always from 1789 his descriptive writing in his Red Books continued and some of them thus reveal his sensitive appreciation of art and nature.

During the lean years he wrote a comedy entitled *Odd Whims* or *Two at a Time* (1783) which Burke enjoyed reading so much he passed it on to Sir Joshua Reynolds. But Reynolds mislaid the manuscript and it was not until a lull in Repton's landscape architecture activities about 1804 that he rewrote it and published it in *Odd Whims and Miscellanies*. Hand-coloured engravings accompanied the work, some of which are to be seen in the Colman collection. His friendship had continued with William Wilkins who had provided the architectural drawings for the early commissions, and it was he who encouraged Repton to rewrite and publish *Odd Whims*. Wilkins was by then controller of several theatres and playhouses in Norfolk and Suffolk; but there is no evidence that Repton's play was ever performed. Among other items in the same publication are 'The Friar's Tale', set in Switzerland, 'One Love' with a Persian setting, and a crazy portrayal of the future of ballooning, 'Voyage to the Moon', in which advice is offered to future aeronauts.

J. C. Loudon records 1803 as the date of an essay on 'Greek and Gothic Architecture' but by 1806 Repton had extended his interest in the expression of architectural style and by the time he presented his proposals to the Prince of Wales for the remodelling of the Pavilion at Brighton he had been strongly drawn towards the Indianesque style. His presentation of this work was masterly and probably represents

43

the apogee of his inventive talent. Permission was granted for its publication in 1809 as *Designs for the Pavillon at Brighton* (Repton used the Middle French word) and it was produced with the acknowledged assistance of both his sons engaged in architecture. He was writing, about the same time, his *Inquiry into the Changes in Taste in Landscape Gardening* and while it was still on the stocks was attacked by Richard Payne Knight in his book *An Analytical Inquiry into the Principles of Taste.* Repton sought recourse in his writing to provide a timely answer. This work stemmed from a commission to update an entry in Miller's *Dictionary of Gardening* on the history of landscape gardening. *Inquiry into the Changes of Taste in Landscape Gardening* was a compilation of parts of the out-of-print *Sketches and Hints* first published in 1795, some of his contribution to the *Dictionary of Gardening* and quotations from *Observations on the Theory and Practice of Landscape Gardening.*

Latterly Repton collected material for his *Fragments on the Theory and Practice of Landscape Gardening* in which he expressed many observations, thoughts and details of work accomplished. Where the Red Books are missing, *Fragments* is invaluable sometimes as evidence of Repton's association with an estate — as for example at Shardeloes in Buckinghamshire.

He ventured to publish a 'Sermon' after the Napoleonic Wars concerning 'the great and sudden change which has brought about deliverance of Europe . . . But the first reverse of fortune', he wrote, 'by which the victor has been vanquished and the destroyer destroyed, was miraculously begun by soft falling flakes of snow, gently scattered like feathers over the surface of the ground, a few days earlier than might naturally be expected . . . and in that same week (Holy Week) has Europe been delivered.'

For a man so closely associated with his pen few letters other than of a business nature remain to reveal his intimate discourse, but in May 1812 he wrote to Thomas Martyn who as Professor of Botany had updated Miller's *Dictionary of Gardening.* Repton was writing from Robertson's Hotel, St Martin's Lane, London, and said: 'The pleasures of life are in our power much oftener than we suppose — and amongst them are the revival of former friendships — so remember it is your fault if ours ever ends. I remain one of your friends.'

Towards the end of his life, overshadowed by the constant threat of sudden death he wrote: 'My ship of life is sinking, and it is time to quit it. I have glided through calms and struggled through tempests, I have touched at every port, and where have we met with happiness unalloyed or where found a man not disappointed? Nowhere! Yet still I must repeat that there is more of good than of evil, and for this redundancy all our gratitude must, at last, resolve itself into that reiterated aspiration from my heart — *Laus Deo.*'

The tomb of Humphry and Mary Repton on the south wall of the parish church at Aylsham, Norfolk.

THE PRINCIPAL EVENTS OF REPTON'S LIFE

1752   Repton born at Bury St Edmunds, Suffolk

1760   *George III became king*

1764   Repton sent to Holland to further his education

1768   Repton apprenticed to the textile trade, in Norwich

1773   Repton married Mary Clarke, at St Mary in Marsh, Norwich

1778   The Reptons moved to the Old Hall, Sustead, near Aylsham

1783   Repton went to Dublin as Secretary to William Windham

1784   Repton joined John Palmer in a scheme to run armed mail coaches

1788   Repton embarked upon his career as a landscape architect

1794-1795   Repton entered into a business partnership with John Nash

1797   Repton achieved royal patronage, and improved the grounds of the Pavilion at Brighton

1799   The agreement with John Nash lapsed

1805   *Battle of Trafalgar*

1806   Repton presented plans for the reshaping of the Pavilion at Brighton

1804   The Horticultural Society (later the Royal Horticultural Society) founded

1808   Repton's proposals for the work at Brighton published by permission of the Prince of Wales.

1810   Repton injured in a carriage accident. His health permanently impaired

1815   *Battle of Waterloo*

1815-1822   Nash redesigned the Pavilion at Brighton and carried out the work

1818   Repton died; buried at Aylsham, Norfolk.

BIBLIOGRAPHY

Humphry Repton; Dorothy Stroud; Country Life, 1962.
A Norfolk Gallery; R. W. Ketton-Cremer; Faber.
The Landscape Gardening and Landscape Architecture of the late Humphry Repton Esq.; J. C. Loudon; 1840.
Parks in England; Hugh Prince; Pinhorn, 1968.
Humphry Repton, Landscape Gardener 1752-1818; George Carter, Patrick Goode and Kedrun Laurie; Sainsbury Centre, Norwich, 1982.

HUMPHRY REPTON'S PUBLISHED WORKS

1781	Contributed the copy and sketches for the Hundreds of North and South Erpingham, in a *History of Norfolk*, 1781 (ten vols.)
1787	*Variety*, a collection of essays; some written by him, others by various friends, anonymously
1788	As an art critic, under a *nom de plume* of The Bee, a contribution to a catalogue on the principles of painting.
1789	A further contribution as The Bee to Boydell's exhibition catalogue.
1794	Letter to Uvedale Price.
1795	*Sketches and Hints* (on Landscape Gardening).
1803	*Observations on the Theory and Practice of Landscape Gardening* (collected from various MSS in the possession of different noblemen and gentlemen). Assisted by his son John Adey Repton FAS.
1804	*Odd Whims and Miscellanies*
1806	*An Inquiry Into the Changes of Taste in Landscape Gardening.*
1808	*Design for the Pavillon at Brighton*, with the assistance of his sons, John Adey Repton and George Stanley Repton, architects.
1810	On the Supposed Effect of Ivy upon Trees (Linnean Society Journal Vol XI, p. 27).
1814	'The Work of Twenty Years brought to a Crisis in Twenty Days' (A sermon, addressed to the fashionable world at the West End of Town).
1816	*Fragments on the Theory and Practice of Landscape Gardening.*

INDEX

Page numbers in italic refer to illustrations